the

FAMILY
Project

John-Paul Flintoff and Harriet Green
Illustrated by Sarah Jane Coleman

First published 2015

by Guardian Books,
Kings Place
90 York Way
London N1 9GU

and Faber & Faber Ltd
Bloomsbury House
74–77 Great Russell Street
London WC1B 3DA

ISBN 978-1-78335-070-4
Text design and layout by The Curved House
Printed and bound by C&C Offset Printing Co. Ltd, China

10 9 8 7 6 5 4 3 2 1

This Book
Belongs To

. . . .

. . . .

. . . .

In every conce
the family is
past, a bridge

able manner,
ur link to our
our future.

Alex Haley

HOW TO USE

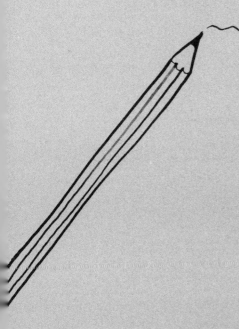

This book is yours.

It will only be worth anything when you have made it your own. We've helped around the edges with some ideas and encouragement. Now your job is to fill in the white spaces – to draw or write or paste things where you like.

Think of the book as a time capsule, crammed with all those interesting things about your family that usually slip unrecorded into the past.

Pack the book with stories and with detail, because these make your family unique. The more you put in, the more valuable it will become – the most wonderful, fact-crammed and heartfelt heirloom imaginable.

So, have you got your pen out yet?

THIS BOOK

YOUR STUFF!

this book ↑

#family

As well as a pen, things you might like to have to hand include pencils, children's crayons, plasticine, felt-tip pens, gold stars and a camera.

Ideally, you will also have access to the internet, so you can upload any work you are proud of.

If you tweet something, use the hashtag #familyproject and we will share it.

project

THE
RULES

This is a handbook for creative discovery,
so feel free to experiment. If you like structure,
here are some rules.

Just tick the ones you agree with.

1. Making a mess may be necessary ☐

2. Mistakes will teach you something ☐

3. Doing it your own way is the right way ☐

4. Sometimes you won't need to think too hard and other times you'll want to delve a bit deeper ☐

5. Some things may be painful, others will be fun ☐

6. Rule-breaking is to be expected ☐

7. It's ok to add other bits of paper, and hold this book together with a rubber band ☐

8. It is your choice whether you share the results of the book with others – or keep it to yourself ☐

(sign here) . . . .

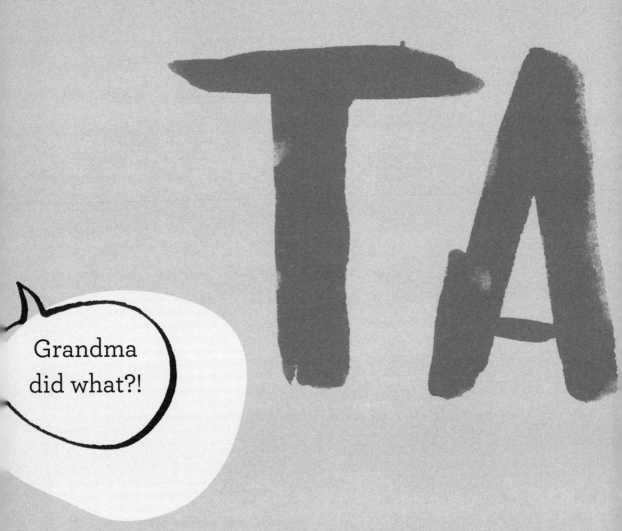

Grandma
did what?!

Even if you don't share this book, it's incredibly
important to collaborate. Talk things through, ask
family, as well as friends. Asking questions will help
you to remember things that matter to you – and
the people you speak to will be glad of the chance
to remember things themselves. Just to help, we'll
remind you, every so often, to get chatting.

Now, let's get started.

All huma[n]
is ONE
UNDIVIDED
INDIVI[SIBLE]

fa[mily]

ity

nd

IBLE

mily.

Mahatma
Gandhi

FAMILY MATTERS BECAUSE:

Different people have different ideas of what
a family is. Anthropologists say one thing,
psychiatrists say another. But in this book, you're the
expert. So, what do you think?

CIRCLE TALKATIVE Abstemious traditional STEA

BAD cooperative words b

Affectionate ANXIOUS Coltish

RESOLUTE SUFFOCATING MIXED-RACE AWARE

majestic Pragmatic INTELLECTUAL TALL mellow ALL RIGHT SAFE

FORTUNATE Artistic TRUTHFUL

connected AWARE absent mischievous BLUN conte Repe

NOISY Clueless BEST cautious

isolated AFRICAN DILIGENT MARVELLOUS!

honourable ethereal BOLD SCOTTISH Po

double-crossing poor INVE

DEPENDENT avant-garde rational COMPLEX Benevolent F

STABLE INFORMAL SAFE PETTY Sneaky a

THRIFTY

SPORTY serious good COMIC HUGGY JEALOUS i

WARM GRUMPY benevolent loopy

Coltish sickly unavoidable FRUGAL co

Jumpy FAIR GOURMET UNITED useless exciting forgetful a

LOVING pushovers courteous hearty LARGE

intolerant DELUDED KOREAN pessimistic KIND HANDSOME STRA

SILLY AVERAGE steadfast MODEST FAIR BITTER

IRISH intuitive easygoing PROUD FAIR BIGHEARTED Welsh

overweight that SURPRISING OUTGOING PATIENT

absent-minded PRAGMATIC musical sentimental

ant old-fashioned LAME

Alcoholic MACABRE Egocentric UNCOMMUNICATIVE

tful FRUGAL SAFE SHARING OUTDOORSY WONKY...

strious generous INTUITIVE NEIGHBOURLY ELEGANT

describe INTUITIVE NORWEGIAN sweet WISE

OUS LUCKY dark-humoured honest

AFFABLE complicated SARCASTIC DULL

CURIOUS slow MEGA

HED UNSIGHTLY HUMBLE DEAFENING

STUPID ticulate BIASED teasing

YOUR accepting BRAVE TRIVIAL

ASSERTIVE SUPERHUMAN COMIC JOLLY

orative genteel tender faithful

laid-back THIN SLOW GLOOMY

ertile riotous short small

lent ORDINARY IMMENSE FAMILY

iligent great! HEALTHY

utterly distant

If you don't know
your family's history,
you don't know anything.
You are a leaf that
doesn't know it is
part of a tree.

Michael Crichton

NOBODY EXISTS IN ISOLATION

To understand your family is to know yourself. The labels we use to describe ourselves – mother, father, sister, brother, daughter, son – only have meaning because somebody else exists, or used to.

And we all have relations – far more of them than we can usually imagine. The further back in the past we look, the more cousins and second- and third-cousins we discover who are living today. And once we become aware of them, they become part of our family – and extend our sense of ourselves.

"I'm trying to do the family tree" can be one of the best excuses for getting in touch with distant cousins.

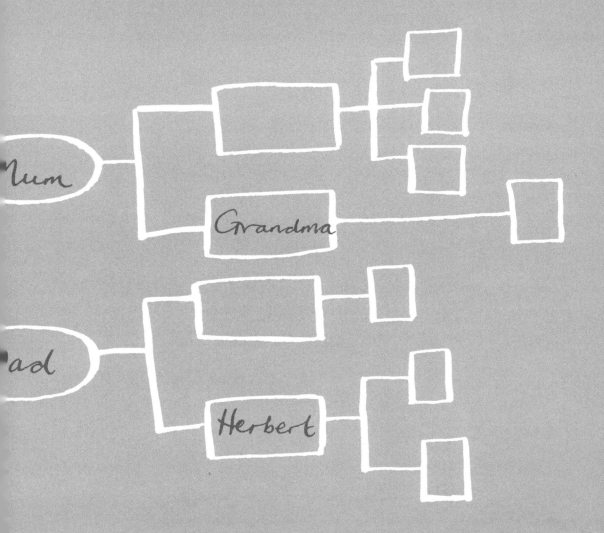

FAMILY TREE

Draw your own here.

Use a pencil, so you can make the ~~corrections~~ ~~correct~~ corrections over time.

If you find the family
tree limiting, with its rigid
structure, try this: draw a
series of concentric circles,
with yourself at the centre, and
place relatives around you according
to how close you feel to them.

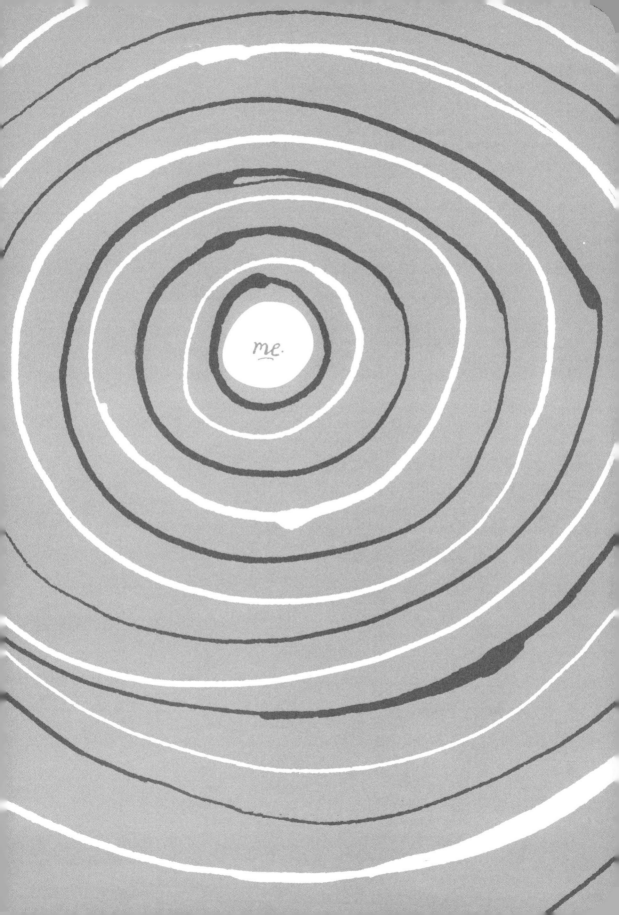

FAMILY CIRCLE

Draw your own here.

FAMILY PHOTOS

Stick in some photos of your family as they are today. Write captions. Include nicknames. Ask distant relatives to send you photos. Put them on these pages and anywhere else you think they are needed.

DRAW or WRITE your

EARLIEST MEMORY

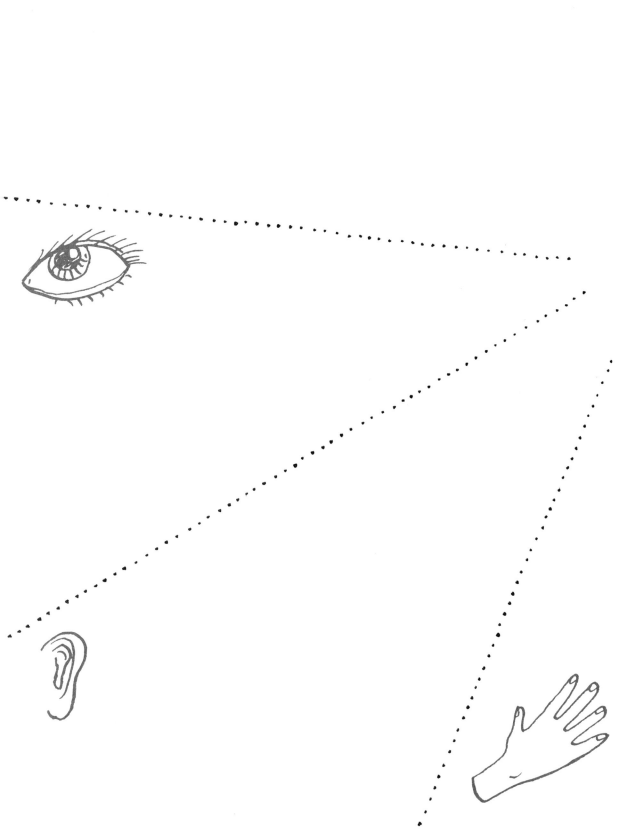

THINK of a TYPICAL
DAY when you were
YOUNGER.
What did you see, hear,
touch, smell and taste?

"Food's ready!"

Draw your family eating together.
Choose a time from long ago.
It doesn't need to be a "good" drawing,
but be sure to include as much detail
as possible.

What's changed?

Draw your family eating together today.
Again, include as much detail as possible.

Favourite Meal

Write down the menu you'd choose. You can pick different courses from different times in your life. Who cooked? Why was it memorable?

Menu

___ starter : ___

___ Main : ___

___ Dessert : ___

___ ☺ ___

Least Favourite Meal

Menu

Starter: ——————

Main: ——————

Dessert: ——————

:(

SHARE YOUR FAMILY RECIPES

Collect your much-loved recipes from family
members. Get them to write the details here.
If that's not possible, try to impersonate
their handwriting.

INGREDIENTS

METHOD

INGREDIENTS

METHOD

INGREDIENTS

METHOD

INGREDIENTS

METHOD

Stuck for space? Add more recipes to the notes section at the back.

ONE THING I LEARNED
from
WATCHING
CHIMPANZEES
is that
having a
CHILD
should be
FUN.

Jane Goodall

Playtime!

What toys or games did you love as a child? Who gave them to you? Who did you play with? Write down or draw what you can remember.

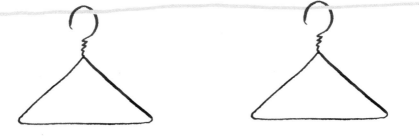

COAT-TALES

Look at old photos. What were you and your family wearing? What clothes did you love and wear to death? Where did they come from?

What books did you read as a child?

Add the names of these books to the spines.

Pick a favourite and write what you remember about the book. If you read it with a parent, ask them to do the same and compare your notes.

Draw the pictures

Add captions, explaining the story behind them
and whether you liked them or not.

rat hung in your HOME

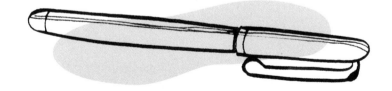

RECORD YOUR Desert Island 'DISCS'

Ask a relative to choose eight favourite pieces of
music. Give them plenty of time in advance to
think. If they need prompts on how to pick their
tracks, give them this list (feel free to add your own
suggestions):

1) Early childhood
2) School
3) Holidays and journeys
4) Being in love
5) People who have died
6) The workplace
7) Things that make you laugh
8) Places you've known

Listen to the tracks together (if you need to, find
them online). Record whatever memories they bring
back. You could do this using audio, like the classic
BBC Radio 4 show *Desert Island Discs*, or just make
written notes. If you record the choices, don't talk for
more than four minutes between tracks, and make a
note here of where the audio can be found.

RE-ENACT AN OLD
FAMILY PHOTO

Stick both the old and new pictures here.

WHO WOULD _YOU_ PUT ON THE PLINTH in TRAFALGAR SQUARE?

Ask your family to nominate the people they admire, and to say why. (It can be anybody, living or dead, fictional or real).

WHO?   PHRASE/PEARL of WISDOM

Do some people in your family say the same things over and over again?
What tends to prompt that? Or are there special phrases that only your
family use? Here is a chance to capture those words, mottos, hard-won bits of
wisdom and (tired) jokes...

PET ZOO

What kinds of animals did your family keep?
Do you remember who actually looked after them
or how they came to join your family? How did
they fit with your family life at the time?

Write an Obituary
for a favourite pet.

Get started: "X, who died aged Y, was…"
Celebrate the most magnificent things about that pet.

Finish with: "X was survived by…" and list
surviving relatives at time of death.

Obituary

GATHER LEAVES,
FLOWERS
- or -
SEEDS
that mean
something
to your
family.

Who has the
green fingers
in your
family?
Where did that
ability come from?

*pierce sellotape
so plants can
dry out.

What special family items were lost, stolen or broken? Ask others for suggestions, so you don't miss anything.

LOST.

(or MISSING, or STOLEN, or BROKEN...)

THINGS WE INHERIT,
THINGS WE PASS ON

Draw the heirlooms you've inherited. While you are
drawing them, think about who you might like to leave
them to in turn.

Be honest and include the heirlooms that you really
didn't want, too.

We inherit our hands from our parents. Each generation holds hands with the next. Look at your hands and think of all the different hands you have held. On this page, draw around them, and around other family members' hands too.

I REALISED

that the clos

looking into

was when I lo

I ever came to
father's eyes

d into
MY SON'S.

Eric Clapton

Do your family share any of these distinguishing features? Nothing familiar? Fill in the blanks.

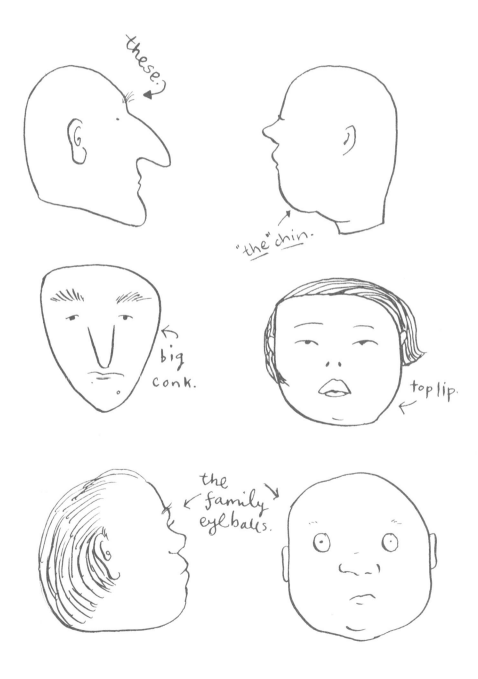

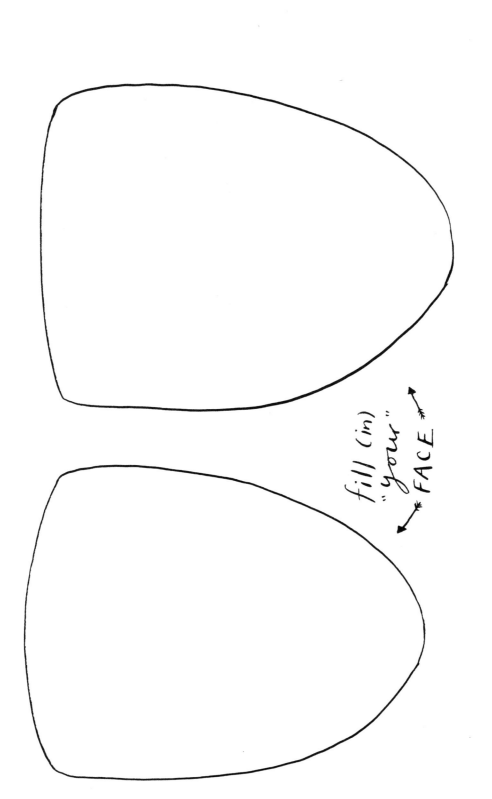

fill (in) "your" FACE

Use these figures to note any inherited health problems, quirks or strengths.

If your great great grandparents cam[e]

see you have plenty of food on

the table? Take photos of things that would STAND -OUTo stay with you what would surprise them about how you live now? Would they be Shocked to see who cooked? Please

In what ways are your family today better off
than previous generations?
And in what ways are they worse off?

STATUS ANXIETY

From our home decor to the shoes we wear,
we all have status symbols. What are yours? Think
about how these things date. Ask your family to
nominate their status symbols and find a way to turn
them into a mini-exhibition.

It is one of
feel closer to dist
the generation i

*re's ways that we often
generations than to
ediately preceding us.*

IGOR STRAVINSKY

WRITE A LETTER
TO FUTURE GENERATIONS

Dear future generation,

Tell them whatever they need to know about you.
Get as many family members to sign the letter as you can.

Yours, ...
(sign here)

BIG NEWS

Write up a family adventure as a news story.
Include headlines, and add pictures.

List all the jobs your family
has done, or dreamt of doing.

actual Jobs.

DREAM JOBS

ASK EVERYONE IN YOUR FAMILY.

OUTSTANDING
~Achievements~

List awards your family members have received.
Local art prize for the under-eights?
Employee of the Month? Include them here. Make
up others you think they deserve.

I don't know who my
Grandfather was;
I am much more
concerned to
know who his
Grandson
will be

Abraham
Lincoln

ASK your FAMILY
to describe what you do

Don't let them compare notes.
Write their answers here.
Do the exercise again for somebody else.

List 50 THINGS
you think are TRUE about another family member.

Include things that are totally random and
"pointless". (Do it in any order and don't check
until later if these facts are correct.)

Now get somebody else to do it about you.

- My sister never cuts her toenails.
-
-
-
-
-
-
-
-
-
-
-
-
-
-
-
-
-
-

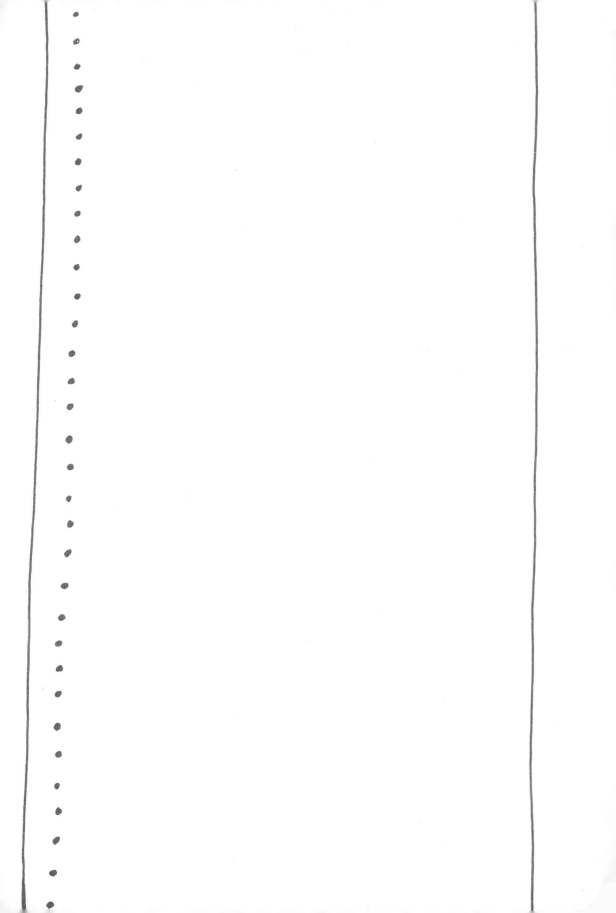

What's your family like with money?

Keep your NOSE OUT! I'm not telling you THAT!

Choose three family members, and plot their (and your) finances over time. We have helped you get started with Mozart's infamous trajectory. Whatever shape you draw, give reasons for the ups and downs (you can make things up).

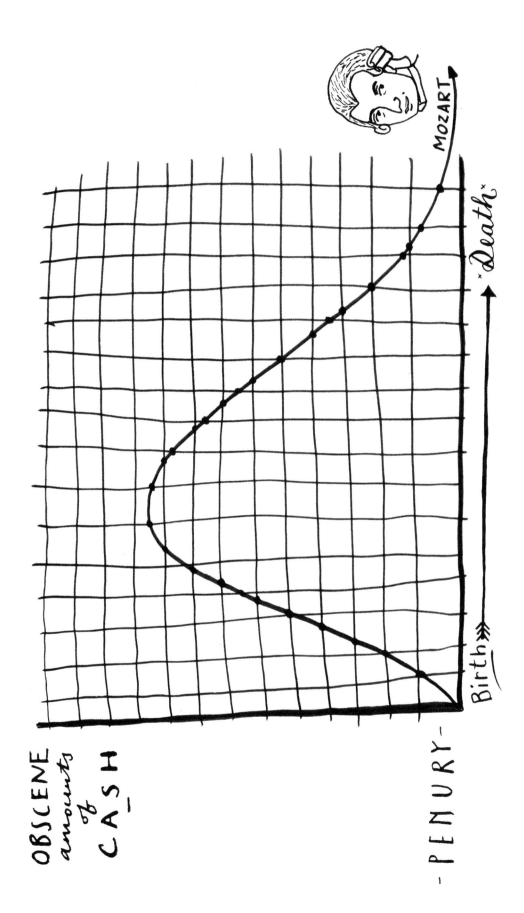

How Competitive Are You?

Think about what you and your family
used to compete over in the past.
What do you compete over now?

COMPETE OVER SOMETHING

RIGHT NOW,
THIS MINUTE.

HAVE A THUMB WAR

PLAY NOUGHTS and CROSSES

ARM WRESTLE

Calculate the distance to your most important relatives. List them here.

Add the distances together, and divide by the number of relatives to calculate the average distance.

Stick different lengths of coloured thread into this book to represent those furthest away and those closest to you.

1   2   3 · 4   5   6   7   8   9   10   11   12   13   14   15   16

20 21 22 23 24 25 26 27 28 29 30 31 32 33 34 35 36

Keep a record of your communications with each of your relatives, over four weeks. Indicate whether by phone, text, social media or other means.

PERSON	CALLS	TEXTS
Mum	I	卌 I

MAILS	SOCIAL MEDIA	other
	卌卌 卌卌 II	

WRITE TO SOMEONE

you've lost touch with,
or who's died.

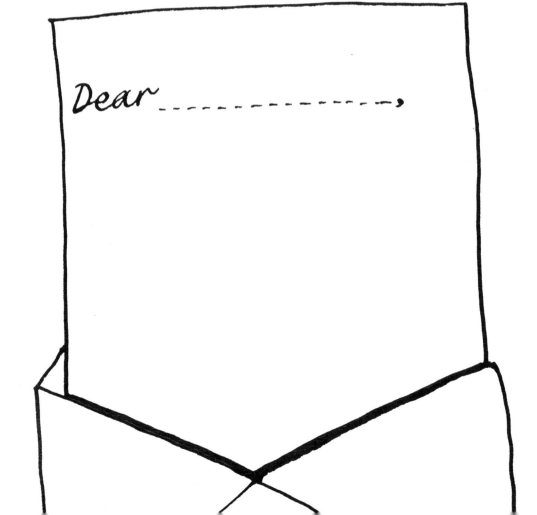

Dear _____,

❤VENN of Love❤

Put your relatives in the appropriate place.

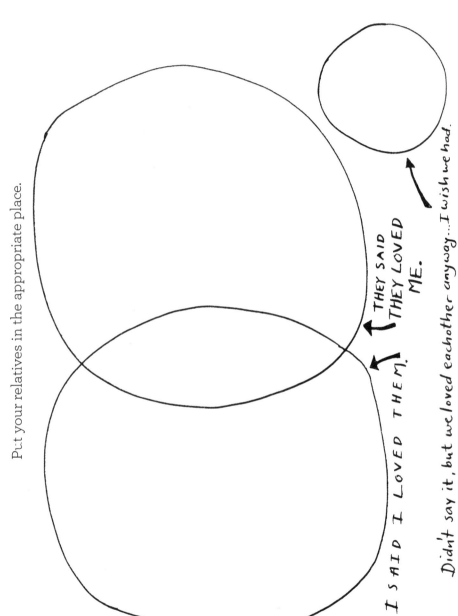

I SAID I LOVED THEM.

THEY SAID THEY LOVED ME.

Didn't say it, but we loved eachother anyway...I wish we had.

List all the ways your family says

"I love you"

This could be in words or actions.

The security of you
really gives you
to think you ca
And

parents' love

foundation

fly.

en you do.

— MICHELLE OBAMA —

TIME TO

When did you stay too long? What relationships, or jobs, or homes did you get stuck in?

GO →

When did you leave too soon? What could have been different if you'd stuck around?

Make a detailed diary of a weekend or a memorable holiday with your family. Record when you came together, and when you separated. Include any tickets, receipts or documents that remind you of that time.

✓ cute.
✓ stripy.
✓ chilly.

A SENSE OF PLACE

"Where are you from?" can be a difficult question. Write some possible answers on this page. Think about specific buildings, neighbourhoods, regions and countries.

How did you get to where you are?

AN ACHE FOR H

lives in all g

where we c

and not BE

ME

us, the safe place

go as we are

ESTIONED.

Maya Angelou

DRAW A MAP OF A PLACE
that's important to SOMEBODY.

Do this exercise together, get as much detail as you can, and write it all down as you go along. You could even create a room plan. It may help to imagine you are in that place right now. Ask: "What's over here?" Capture specifics so that, if you had to, you could build an accurate, full-sized replica. If they mention trees, ask what species. If there's a light fitting, what did it look like? But it's not just about facts. Ask what they felt about the things they describe, and what was important about them.

- CHILDHOOD JOURNEYS -

Think of the routes you took – to school, clubs,
shops, relatives' houses. Use different colours for
different trips. Work on an old map, or find one
online, or just draw from memory. Note the main
landmarks, big or small.

*For best results, do this with
the people who accompanied you
at the time.

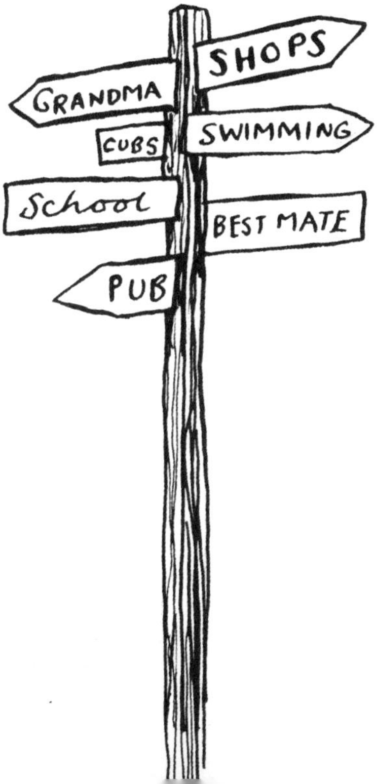
SHOPS
GRANDMA
CUBS
SWIMMING
School
BEST MATE
PUB

How SETTLED are you?

are you?

Where do you fit on this spectrum? Are you an un-budgeable boulder? Or a barnacle? Perhaps a caged bird or a tethered goat? Or more of a migrating swallow or a hyperactive housefly?

And where do your relatives belong? Add them, giving reasons – and feel free to invent your own metaphors.

goat.
(in case you were wondering).

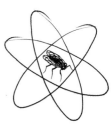

MAP OF LOVE

How did your parents end up together? Think of the key milestones and turning points, and use the full page to show how those gradually led them towards (and perhaps away from) each other. Connect these points using arrows (straight or wobbly as you see fit).

If they have separated, plot that too.

INTREPID
TRAVELLERS

How much did your grandparents travel? And your
parents? And you? Or your children?

List the really important journeys in your family.

What made them important? How were individuals
changed by them?

Find postage stamps from the places and times
involved, and write your answers beside them. The
stamps don't need to be rare or expensive. Find
them online, print them and stick them in here. Or
draw replicas instead.

1

2

3

4

5

6

7

8

9

10

FAMILY Holiday!

List ten lessons, big or small, that you learned on
travels with your immediate family.

WHAT I LEARNED.

1

 2

3

 4

5

 6

7

 8

9

 10

The greatest
family is th
of the pare

gedy of the
unlived lives
ts.

CARL GUSTAV JUNG

Any regrets?

What were your parents' missed opportunities?
Were they willing sacrifices? What price did they
pay? If you can, ask them!

And what about you?

FAMILY EVENTS ☺

Great Grandma
Jones Born
✳

WORLD EVENTS 🌐

WWI
●

1914

eg: ——→

↑ Enter Dat

YOUR FAMILY, THROUGH TIME

Create a timeline, showing what events
your family lived through.

ng this line

TIME TRAVELLERS

Imagine meeting one of your parents at exactly the age you are now. What would you do? What would you talk about? Think about the kinds of advice, or jokes, you could swap. Write it up as a script, or draw it as a comic.

Do the same for your other parent, or someone else you love a lot. If you run out of space, use the notes section at the back of the book.

How did you come to believe the things you believe,
in politics or religion? Draw a family tree to show
what you inherited from whom.

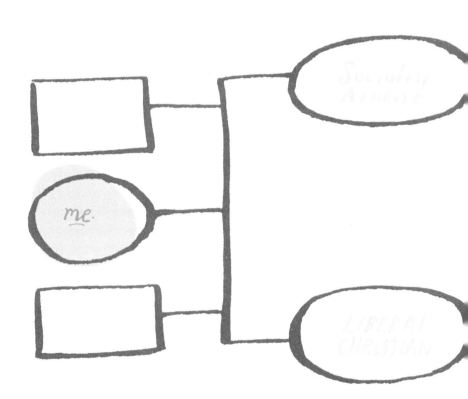

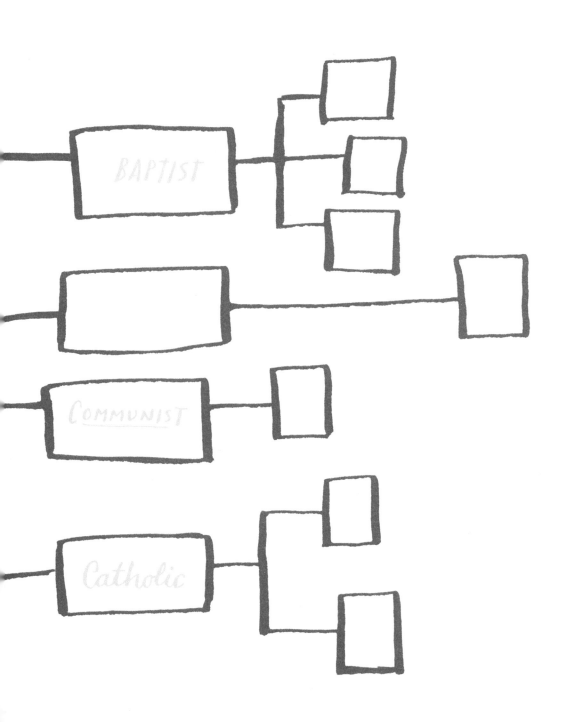

No mirror eve

No bread eve

No ripened grape eve

Mature yourself and b

from

ecame iron again;
ecame wheat;
ecame sour fruit.
cure
ange for the worse.

MEVLANA RUMI

DESCRIBE HOW YOU CELEBRATE BIRTHDAYS

TYPICALLY. | NOT so WELL. | AT BEST.

Draw up a plan for the next family birthday.
Be sure to include baking a cake. Stick a photo or
drawing of the day (and your cake) in here.

(family
plates
– never matched)

BIRTHDAY

(and
the
rest)

Design a way to mark your COMING of AGE

In a secular age, many rites of passage have
changed. Ask your parents or grandparents how
they marked their coming of age. How would you
mark yours if you could have it your own way?
Include both privileges and responsibilities.

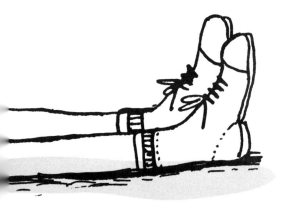

BLAZE of GLORY

Design your own funeral. Ask others how they
would like to go. Make notes!

Have you ever spoken of this before? What happens
when you raise the idea?

...how much

influence

do the

dead

have?

... how much would you like them to have?

LIST 10 FAMILY
MYSTERIES

Start with tiny ones ("Why do socks always go missing?") and allow more significant ones to emerge. Is it important to solve them, or just bring them to light?

The universe is full of magical things patiently waiting for our wits to grow sharper

EDEN PHILPOTTS

What are your family secrets?

Why are or were they secret? Who kept them? What might have happened if they got out? How many secrets do you keep?

Write a secret here. Staple the pages together.

If you dare, ask a relative "what don't I know about you?"

(sssh! Don't talk about that!)

What arguments do you remember?
Plot them on this graph.

SEVERITY

Volcanic

"EARTH" mover

UGLY

CALM

- AGES AGO -

WHEN

- RECENT -

Choose a disagreement that you've all put behind you. Each person should write down their own position and feelings at the time. Write in the present tense.

Pass your version to (one of) the other participant(s) in that argument. Each person is to read the other's statement, without passing comment or pulling silly faces.

Now each sign the certificate to show it really is the end of all that.

Certificate of Making-Up

- FROM THE OFFICE OF DISPUTE RESOLUTION -

(sign here) . . . .

DATE:	PRESENT:	FAMILY CONSTABULARY
TIME:		

WITNESS STATEMENT

DATED: _ _ _ _ _ _ _ _ _ _ _

WITNESS: _ _ _ _ _ _ _ _ _ _ _ _ _ _ _ _ _

OVERSEEING OFFICER: _ _ _ _ _ _ _ _ _ _ _

CLERK: _ _ _ _ _ _ _ _ _ _ _ _ _ _ _ _ _

Think of a moment in your family's past that had a big impact. (Not an argument!)

Record your own recollection. You could write it down, but for greater impact use video or audio. Then record somebody else's account. Don't pass any comment while you are doing this. The idea is not to look for who is "right", but to celebrate the differences.

WHAT CAN YOU DO
TO PROMOTE
WORLD PEACE?

Go home
and love
your family.

Mother Teresa

WHAT DO YOU

ESPECIALLY LIKE

ABOUT YOUR RELATIONS?

NAME	CHARACTERISTIC	When that was DEMONSTRATED

WHAT,
AS A FAMILY MEMBER,
are your
OWN STRENGTHS?

List at least ten. (Put modesty aside.)

Assumptions are the termites of relationships.

HENRY WINKLER

We are gathered here today...

Marriage vows are explicit, and provide a measure of how couples get on. But most of our relationships rest on unspoken assumptions.

What agreements could you make with others?

Moments of GENIUS

When has your family made you burst with pride? When has somebody said something that sounded like genius? Or done something wonderfully characteristic, or brilliantly out of character?

Write any moments you can think of on separate pieces of paper. Roll up the paper and tie with cotton thread. Store in a jar labeled "Magic". Use a big jar, so there's room for more magic in the future.

What next?

Throw a family party to celebrate completing this book.
Stick pictures of the party in here, please!

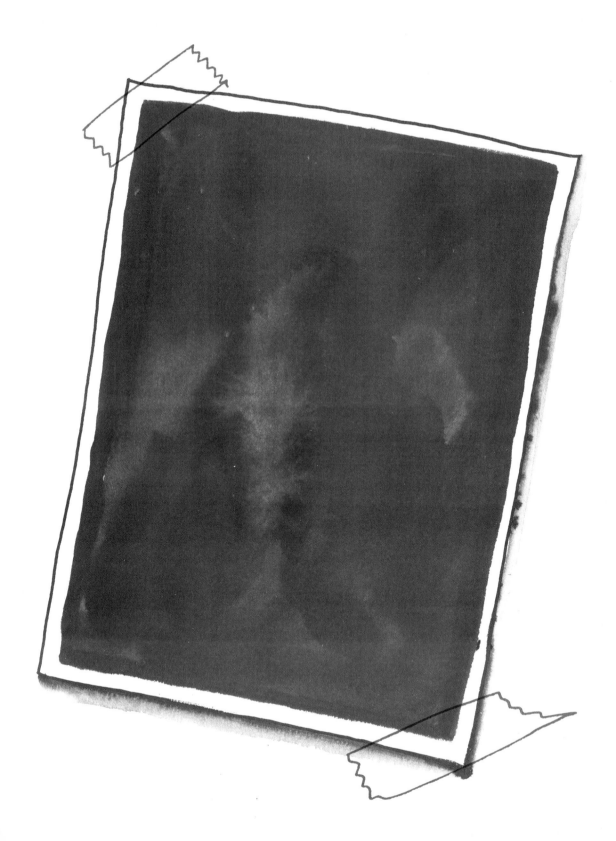

WHO is WHO?

At your party, make sure to get everybody to leave their mark in this book.

Provide an ink pad so they can put in a thumbprint. Ask them to turn the thumbprint into a self-portrait, and write their name beneath it.

NAME:

NAME:

PRESS

NAME:

NAME:

NAME:

NAME:

NAME:

NAME:

NAME:

NAME:

NAME:

NAME:

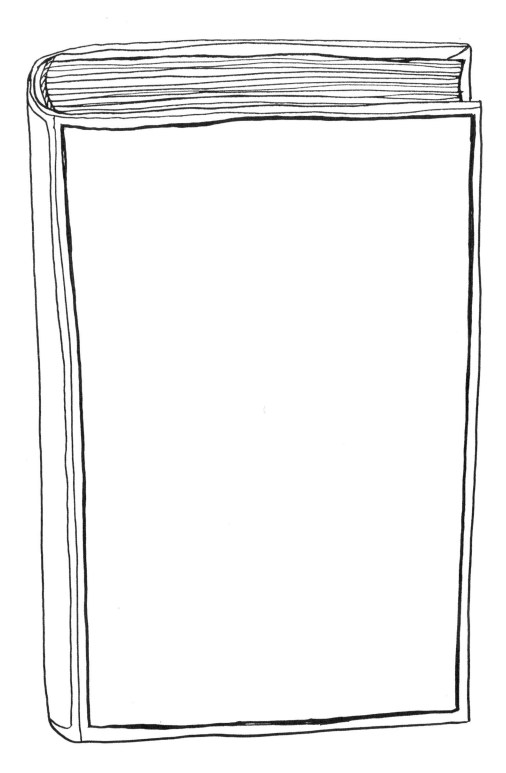

What would be the title of your

Family Memoir♡?

Choose the title you like best, and design a new cover for this Family Project. You'll need a piece of A3 paper to give you room to wrap it around the book. Just for now, you can draw the title on the picture over here.

· ABOUT US ·

We're married, with a daughter, and a vast, shared family tree.

John-Paul is a writer, artist and film-maker. For years he edited and wrote features for the *Financial Times* and the *Sunday Times*. His book, *How To Change The World*, is published in fourteen languages worldwide. A fully trained life coach, he teaches creativity at the School of Life, in London and elsewhere.

@jpflintoff

As editor of the *Guardian*'s Family section, Harriet commissions and edits startling, moving stories about families every week. She's an award-winning feature writer and has previously worked as deputy editor of *Harper's Bazaar* and at the *Daily Telegraph*.

@harrietrgreen

note
to
self.